The Sun Above
and the
River Below

Wes Magee
Illustrated by Kate McKeon

Rigby

A Harcourt Achieve Imprint

www.Rigby.com
1-800-531-5015

Literacy by Design Leveled Readers: *The Sun Above and the River Below*

ISBN-13: 978-1-4189-3793-5
ISBN-10: 1-4189-3793-2

Printed in China
3 4 5 6 7 8 985 14 13 12 11 10 09 08

Contents

**How the Sun Came
to Be in the Sky**................................. 5

**How the Niagara Falls
Were Created**................................... 27

How the Sun Came to Be in the Sky
A Kiowa Indian Tale

Saynday, a trickster man, lived in the rocky desert on the dark side of the world. He carried a snake stick with him wherever he went. One day Saynday came across a fox looking miserable.

"What troubles you, Fox?" asked Saynday.

"It's this darkness," replied Fox. "There is no light on this side of the world, and so nothing grows. There are no flowers, and the trees are bare. It's dark all the time, and it's so, so cold."

Sayday nodded, and said, "This is how it's always been, since the time of my father, and my father's father. We have always lived in the darkness."

Fox followed Sayday as he continued to walk across the rocky desert. Soon they reached the bank of a dark, swirling river. There they met a deer.

Deer looked unhappy.

"What troubles you, Deer?" asked Sayday.

Deer sadly moaned, "It's the darkness. There's never any light, and it's cold, and–"

"–nothing grows, right?" interrupted Fox. "I know what you mean."

"So do I," a voice cawed. "I hate it here in the dark."

Fox spun around. "Who said that?" he demanded.

"I did," the voice answered.

Sayday, Fox, and Deer peered into the darkness, but they couldn't see anyone.

"I'm up here," the voice cawed again. Saynday looked up and saw a crow perched on the branch of a leafless tree. "You're feeling miserable because of this never-ending darkness, right?" he asked.

"Terribly miserable," said Crow.

Saynday sat on the bank of the dark river and thoughtfully poked the ground with his snake stick. He looked over at the gloomy fox, the unhappy deer, and the cranky crow. At last he spoke.

"I have the answer! I know where we can find light and warmth," he told the three creatures.

"Like where . . . *where?*" cried Fox.

Saynday told them about the Sun People who lived on the other side of the world.

The Sun People owned a beautiful Sun Ball that gave endless light and warmth, and Saynday told how the Sun People all gathered together in a wide field outside their village once every year. There was feasting and celebrating, and late in the afternoon, the Sun People brought out the Sun Ball to play a special game.

"What *is* this game?" asked Crow.

"The old Sun People play against the young Sun People," explained Saynday, "and whichever team manages to capture the Sun Ball wins the game."

"It all sounds very interesting," said Deer sadly, "but how will it help us get rid of this everlasting dark and cold?"

"I've got a plan," the clever Saynday said, smiling and tapping the side of his nose with a long finger. "Now listen carefully, everyone."

After they'd listened to Saynday's plan, the three creatures agreed that it was indeed very clever. They waved goodbye to Saynday as they headed off to the Sun People's village.

"Remember to follow my instructions," Saynday called after them. "While you're gone, I'm going to stay here and build myself a wooden hut."

Fox, Deer, and Crow crossed the rocky desert and climbed a chain of hills, stopping to rest on top of the highest one.

They gazed down on a wonderful sight. They stood in silence until Fox exclaimed, "Would you look at *that*!"

"It's amazing!" murmured Deer.

"It's beautiful!" cawed Crow.

It was a world of light, just like Saynday said.

In the center of the wide field, they saw the Sun Ball, which shone and sparkled, glowed and gleamed! Sunbeams, like long streamers, waved and swayed into the air. Even at a distance, the three animals could feel the warmth coming from the Sun Ball.

"OK, guys," said Fox at last, "it's time to put Saynday's plan into action. Wish me luck!"

"Good luck," said Deer and Crow.

Fox ran down the side of the hill and soon reached the Sun People's village. The Sun People stopped feasting and celebrating. They stared at their visitor.

"Who are *you*?" an old woman asked.

"I'm Fast Fox, and I'm here to play the game," Fox replied.

"Then you're just in time," one of the young Sunnies told him, "because the game starts later this afternoon. It's the old Sunnies against the young Sunnies."

The Sun People were very friendly, and Fox soon got to know everyone. He ate and drank with them and enjoyed the food very much. The old Sunnies explained how the young Sunnies won the game every year.

"Why's that?" asked Fox.

"Because they're younger and stronger and faster," the old Sunnies told him. "It's not fair!"

Fox thought for a moment and then said, "Maybe I can help."

"How?" asked the old Sunnies.

Fox said, "I'm as fast as the wind and quick as lightning. With my speed I can help you win the game."

"Great!" shouted the old Sunnies excitedly.

Fox smiled to himself, thinking that Saynday's clever plan was working—at least so far.

When it was time for the game to start, Fox joined the old Sunnies at one end of the wide field, while the young Sunnies gathered at the other end. They looked faster and stronger than the old Sunnies, that's for sure.

Placed between the two teams was the Sun Ball, which shone and sparkled, glowed and gleamed. It cast its light and warmth across the entire field. A few minutes later, a whistle blew, and the game began.

The young Sunnies ran and pushed. The old Sunnies shoved and dove for the ball. The two teams pulled the sunbeam streamers this way and that way, all in an effort to capture the Sun Ball.

Fox ran alongside the old Sunnies on his team, but he never tried to get the Sun Ball–not yet. He had to be patient and wait for his chance.

The younger players were very strong and fast, just like the old Sunnies had said. With their extra strength, they easily knocked the old Sunnies out of the way. They kicked the Sun Ball downfield, well out of reach of the older players.

Fox watched every move and finally, during a pause in the game, he saw his chance.

Fast as the wind and quick as lightning, Fox slipped between two players and grabbed the longest sunbeam streamer in his teeth, then he raced away across the field, pulling the Sun Ball behind him.

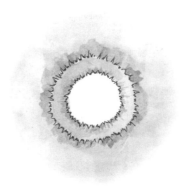

"Run, Fox, run!" shouted the old Sunnies in excitement.

"Hey, come back here, Fox!" roared the young Sunnies, and they set off after the speedy fox.

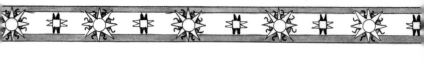

With the Sun Ball streamer firmly gripped in his teeth, Fox headed out of the valley, racing at top speed and leaving the young Sunnies far, far behind.

17

Fox was exhausted by the time he reached the top of the hill. "Your turn now, Deer!" he panted.

Deer hoisted the Sun Ball onto his antlers and took off across the hills, followed by Fox and Crow. He didn't stop until he reached the rocky desert.

"Your turn now, Crow!" he shouted.

Crow grabbed the sunbeam streamer in her beak and flew up and up, gliding high above the rocky desert. Soon she reached the dark, swirling river. The Sun People had chased the three animals for as long as they could, but they were much too slow to keep up. Before long, the Sun People gave up the chase.

Crow landed on the riverbank, right next to Saynday's newly-built wooden hut. A short time later, Fox and Deer arrived, panting and breathless.

"You sly creatures!" Saynday cried. "You captured the Sun Ball! Tell me, did everything go according to plan? Did you

play their game? And did you sneak the Sun Ball away like I told you?"

"Yes, indeed! It was a very clever plan," said Fox.

Saynday nodded knowingly and tapped the side of his nose with a long finger.

The Sun Ball brought instant light and warmth to the dark side of the world. The waters of the swirling river sparkled like a million mirrors, leaves began to grow on the trees, flowers bloomed, and all seemed well with the world.

A few weeks later Fox, Deer, and Crow knocked on the door of Saynday's wooden hut.

"How are you today, my friends?" asked Saynday. "Are you enjoying the warmth and light?"

"That's what we're here about," said Fox. "The Sun Ball never shuts off!"

"We can't sleep," moaned Deer.

"And the plants and leaves just keep on growing and growing and growing," cawed Crow.

Saynday thoughtfully scratched his head, then banged his snake stick on the ground. "Here is my plan. If I were to put the Sun Ball inside my hut, the light would only shine through the cracks in the walls."

"That's right," agreed Fox.

"That would give the world light *and* shade," explained Saynday.

"Sounds good to us," said Fox, Deer, and Crow, and together they rolled the Sun Ball inside Saynday's wooden hut.

As clever Saynday had said, light shone through the cracks in the walls. This meant that there wasn't too much light or too much dark. The three creatures were able to sleep, and the plants didn't grow quite so quickly. Saynday, the trickster man, had once again found the answer to the problem.

But something wasn't right.

The heat from the Sun Ball was so strong that the wooden walls of Saynday's hut grew hotter and hotter, until finally the wood began to smoke. Suddenly, the walls burst into flame, and within minutes, Saynday's newly-built wooden hut was nothing but ashes.

Saynday was angry—in fact, he was *furious*!

In a terrible rage, Saynday grabbed the longest sunbeam streamer and began to swing the Sun Ball above his head. Around and around and around, faster and faster and faster, he whirled the Sun Ball.

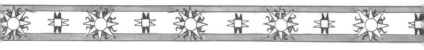

Saynday let go of the streamer, and
the Sun Ball flew high into the blue sky.
And that's where it stayed. It would never
come down again.

Not only that, but Saynday had been
so angry, and he'd thrown the Sun Ball
so hard, that it sailed through the sky
to the other side of the world that lay
to the west. There was darkness again,
but soon the Sun Ball came sailing back,
rising from the east. Forever after, the Sun
passed through the sky to set in the
west, and every morning it rose again
in the east.

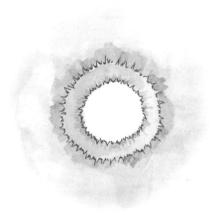

This meant that the land of the rocky desert would never again have too much light, or too much dark. And Fox, Deer, and Crow were very happy because they could finally get a good night's sleep.

And as for Saynday . . . Well, he built himself another wooden hut. Every day, the trickster man sat on the bank of the swirling, sparkling river and looked up at the Sun Ball shining in the sky. He banged his snake stick on the ground, smiled, and nodded knowingly.

All's well with the world, he thought, and he tapped the side of his nose with a long finger.

And that is how the Sun came to be in the sky.

How the Niagara Falls Were Created

An Iroquois Indian Tale

Long, long ago, a snake named Manda lived in a cave in the far North. Each day, she slithered out from her home and fed on grass for hours and hours. And each day, Manda grew larger and larger, until she wasn't just a regular-sized, green snake—she was a huge, green snake! And yet, she kept eating, for she had no fears that she would ever run out of grass.

As the years passed, however, the weather in the far North turned terribly cold, and chilly winds howled down from the snow-capped mountains. Winter had come, and it showed no signs of leaving.

The weather steadily worsened, the land became covered in ice and snow, and the grass withered and died.

Manda shivered in her cave. With no grass for her to eat, she grew hungrier and hungrier. There was still no sign of spring, so the huge, green snake had no choice but to find a new home.

She slithered across the frozen snow and slowly, very slowly, made her way south.

Day after day, Manda traveled on. The days turned into weeks, and Manda continued to slither further and further south in search of food and a new home.

At long last, after a journey taking many months, the weather grew warmer, and Manda left the snows far behind. She reached the lands of the far South, where it was warm all year long.

Feeling tired and very hungry, the snake stopped to rest beside a river whose waters boiled and bubbled as they swept around sharp rocks. On the other side of the river, Manda saw a wide plain covered in green grass.

"If only I could cross this wild river," Manda said, "I would be able to eat all I wanted, and maybe, just maybe, I'd find a new cave where I could sleep."

But how could she cross such a wide and dangerous river?

The huge, green snake slithered down the riverbank until she discovered a rope bridge strung across the water. The river's wild waters boiled and bubbled below.

Nervously, very nervously, Manda began to slither her long body across the wobbling, swaying rope bridge. She was so large and so long, that when her head had reached the other side, her tail had yet to start its dangerous journey across the swaying bridge!

Manda was a little shaken and scared, but she breathed a huge hiss of relief when her long body was safely on the other side.

Without delay, Manda settled down on the grassy plain and began feasting—oh yes, the green grass was delicious! She was so hungry that she ate nonstop for ten days and ten nights, singing to herself:

This grass is so yummy,
I must fill my tummy!
Delicious blades of green,
More than I've ever seen!
I'll eat and never stop.
I'll eat until I pop.

And so it happened that a fisherman and his two children came to fish at the wild river and spied the huge, green snake feasting on the grassy plain.

"Wow, just look at the size of that huge, green snake!" cried the man in open-mouthed amazement.

"I've never seen a snake that huge or green," said the girl nervously.

Her small brother worriedly said, "Perhaps it's dangerous. We should get back to the village and warn everyone!"

The fisherman and his two children ran back to their village, gasping, "We've seen a huge, green snake!"

"Where?" asked the villagers.

"It's on the grassy plain, beside the wild river!" exclaimed the fisherman's son.

"What's it doing there?" demanded the chief of the village.

"Eating all the grass," the fisherman told him. "She's big . . . and getting even bigger!"

The villagers stopped in their tracks and stared at him.

"Now, let's not be foolish," the chief told them. "The snake doesn't look that bad, does it? After all, it is only eating grass, and I actually think it looks, well, quite harmless, even friendly!"

The villagers held a discussion and agreed that the huge, green snake didn't look that threatening. And so a man and a woman volunteered to approach the creature. Watched by young and old alike, the two brave villagers slowly made their way across the grassy plain.

They stopped a short distance away, shading their eyes from the sun in order to see the snake more clearly. They noticed that up close, the creature looked even longer and fatter than before. Manda, meanwhile, stared back at the two villagers, munching another mouthful of grass.

After a few minutes, the villagers and the huge, green snake exchanged nervous nods, so the two villagers felt brave enough to step closer.

"You're not, er, dangerous, are you?" they asked. "You only eat grass, don't you?"

For a moment Manda looked puzzled, then her mouth opened and she gave the two villagers a wide smile. Still feeling slightly nervous, the man and the woman walked up to the snake and patted her green skin.

"Come and see for yourselves," called the woman in excitement.

All the villagers ran forward, and within minutes everyone was patting and stroking the huge, green snake's skin.

Manda loved this tickling business, and she delighted the villagers with her wide smile and low, rumbling laugh.

"We'll adopt her," declared the chief. "She will be our new pet!"

All the villagers clapped and cheered.

And so Manda became the villagers' pet and moved to the village, where she slept on the ground at night and slithered out onto the grassy plain each day to eat her fill of green grass.

Of course, the huge, green snake grew even longer and fatter. She had been huge before, but now she was super huge! Manda was very happy in her new home. The bitterly cold and snowy lands of the far distant North were long, long forgotten. At last Manda was content. She didn't mind sleeping outside on the ground, but she missed her cave and wished she could find a new cave home.

The villagers noticed that as the weeks passed Manda didn't smile as wide as she used to. She didn't laugh with her low, rumbling laugh either when they tickled her. It was clear that the huge, green snake wanted a house of some kind—a private place where she could curl up and sleep peacefully.

"I know a cave," suggested the village fisherman. "She might like it there."

"That's just what Manda needs," the chief said. "Snakes like to live in caves, where they have a cool place to sleep out of the sun."

The villagers all nodded in agreement. "Where is this cave?" they asked.

"Beside the wild river," the fisherman told them.

"Take us there and show us the cave," ordered the chief.

The fisherman led the villagers—and Manda—to the wild river, where he pointed out a deep, dark cave.

Manda smiled her widest smile yet,
thinking this could be her dream home.
She gave a low, rumbling laugh, then she
slithered into the deep, dark cave, curled
up, and fell sound asleep.

Manda had found friendly and helpful villagers, an endless supply of green grass, and a new home. What more could a huge, green snake want?

For many years Manda fed on grass from the plain and continued to grow until her cave home became too small for her. She was so long that her head stuck out the front. She was so wide that she had to stack her coils on top of each other until she reached the ceiling.

She had no choice but to make room for herself—so she started digging and throwing loose dirt and rocks out of the cave.

She threw lots and lots of rocks into the wild river, and over time the loose rocks piled up and up.

Meanwhile, Manda continued to eat and get larger. In order to fit into her cave, she had to throw out even more rocks. As the days passed, she threw out hundreds and hundreds of loose rocks . . . then thousands . . . then tens of thousands.

The more rocks Manda dug out of her cave, the more she threw into the river, and the higher the pile of river rocks grew. The rock pile filled the river until it blocked it completely.

The river's waters boiled and bubbled as they rose higher, roaring and foaming until at last the wild river poured over the tall wall of rock and crashed down, down, down.

The tumbling water plunged over the cliff, and before long it became a beautiful waterfall to which generation after generation of villagers came to stand and stare in amazement.

No one could remember exactly when it happened, but at some point, the opening to Manda's cave home became lost behind the waterfall's white mist of fine spray.

After that the huge, green snake was never seen again.

Today, visitors from around the world visit the waterfall Manda built, standing in silence and gazing in wonder at the power and size of this amazing sight.

Only a few people know the story of Manda, and those who do wonder if the huge, green snake still sleeps in her cave, hidden somewhere behind the waterfall's white mist of fine spray. They pause and think for a moment about the creature that came from the bitter cold of the snowy North . . . and how she created the world-famous Niagara Falls.